Manifest Your Year

12-MONTH PERPETUAL PLANNER

Laura Chung

UNION
SQUARE
& CO.

NEW YORK

**UNION
SQUARE
& CO.**

NEW YORK

ISBN 978-1-4549-4960-2

For information about custom editions, special sales, and premium
purchases, please contact specialsales@unionsquareandco.com.

Printed in China

2 4 6 8 10 9 7 5 3 1

unionsquareandco.com

Cover and interior design by Melissa Farris
Image Credits: Srgr/Shutterstock.com

Introduction

Manifesting is the process of you co-creating your life with a Higher Power. It is a work of art created by that co-creation: a combination of how you live and the expression of your love for something that is important to you. This love could find its shape in a career, a legacy, or some other kind of purpose. It's the intention that drives you forward every day. When you offer it to the world, you are giving something that is incredibly important to you. In exchange, you will receive everything you need—automatically. That is because giving and receiving are one and the same. It's a fact of nature. It's a universal law.

This perpetual planner—which can be used as a companion to my book, *How to Manifest: Make Your Dreams a Reality in 40 Days,* or on its own—is about peeling back the layers of yourself. When we let go of expectations, there is no limit to the unique beauty that we can find in ourselves as we begin to understand our strongest personal motivations.

I offer my own unique perspective on manifestation, one that encompasses both Eastern and Western philosophies. It includes practices and ideas from my studies in psychology, quantum physics, energy healing, the universal laws, and astrology to help guide you in co-creating your dream life from a place of wholeness.

My intention for this planner is to share my knowledge and wisdom with you on how to co-create your dream life with a Higher Power. You can call this Higher Power a Life Force Energy, the Force, the Universe, God, Goddess, Spirit, or the Divine. It is the energy in all things.

Each week, you will read the lesson for the day and do the practice, and often journal about it. On the right-hand pages, you can fill in the month at the top of the page, and then the date and day of the week before each slash. The circles at the end of each line represent the moon phases; you can fill them in depending on the date.

The intention of this whole journey is to have fun and enjoy the process. My wish for you is that if you get anything out of this book, it will be an ability to shift your beliefs and see your present circumstances in a different way.

We are in the business of healing the past, shaking off limiting perceptions, and getting rid of a belief in scarcity. And together, we'll not only improve your life and your ability to pursue your dreams but also add joy, peace, healing, and abundance to this world. I believe that when more of us feel this way, we'll gain the ability to change the world in new and powerful ways.

**The Universe
doesn't give you
what you want,
it gives you who you are,
and sometimes
it takes time until you
are ready for it.**

Week 1

"Every moment is the manifestation of the whole.
Life itself is, therefore, nothing but the continuous
moment of the whole."
—Yamada Koun, *The Gateless Gate*

What Is Manifestation?

I believe the key to happiness is to feel grateful for your present circumstances but also have a deep knowing that you can change your circumstances at any time with your thoughts, feelings, and your will. Manifesting at the macro level is being in alignment with who you really are. At the micro level, people manifest to feel good—material manifestations that are attached to a perceived emotion. The object of your desire gives you a momentary serotonin boost, and then you are in a hamster wheel of manifesting. While I'm not saying you shouldn't manifest these things, it will be to your benefit to be in the flow with your life. To understand yourself at the micro and macro level. Being in the flow versus forcing. Trusting versus controlling. Write below what manifestation means to you:

_____

_____

_____

_____

_____

_____

_____

_____

_____

_____

Month

Date/Day of Week   **Moon Phase**

_____/_____ ◯

_____/_____ ◯

_____/_____ ◯

_____/_____ ◯

_____/_____ ◯

_____/_____ ◯

_____/_____ ◯

Week 2

"Your life is the manifestation of your dream; it is an art. And you can change your life anytime if you're not enjoying the dream."
—Don Miguel Ruiz, *The Four Agreements*

What Have You Manifested?

Write about some things that you've successfully manifested, whether you realized it or not at the time. Take note of what you thought of while you did it. Did you have a vision board? (See week 4 for how to make one.) How quickly did your manifestations come to you? Did they come in the form that you had intended? Whenever I review the manifestations that I have called into being, the exercise reminds me that I've been able to manifest before. And if I have done it before, I can do it again!

_____

_____

_____

_____

_____

_____

_____

_____

_____

_____

_____

_____

_____

Month

Date/Day of Week

Moon Phase

Week 3

"Visualizing is a mental process governed by the reasoning or conscious mind; visioning is a spiritual process, governed by intuition, or the superconscious mind."

—Florence Scovel Shinn,
The Complete Works of Florence Scovel Shinn

Envisioning Reality

As creative beings, we have the power to envision our lives. If you want or desire something in your life and you don't have it, you can close your eyes and imagine yourself in a different reality. We have the power to dream something better for ourselves with our creative and imaginative minds. Here are some journal prompts that you can use.

- What kind of job or career do you want?
- Do you want to be your own boss?
- Do you want flexible working hours?
- What do your days look like?
- What kind of lifestyle do you want?
- What do your health and wellness look like?
- What do your relationships and love look like?
- What kind of clothes do you wear?
- How do you feel?
- Where do you live?

_____

_____

_____

_____

_____

_____

Month

_____

Date/Day of Week   ## Moon Phase

_____/_____   ◯

_____/_____   ◯

_____/_____   ◯

_____/_____   ◯

_____/_____   ◯

_____/_____   ◯

_____/_____   ◯

Week 4

"Vision is the Art of seeing Things invisible."
—Jonathan Swift, "Thoughts on Various Subjects"

Making Your Vision Board

Consider incorporating visual representations of your answers into a vision board. You'll need a poster board, magazines, scissors, markers, glue and/or tape. Put on some good music and drink some tea or other good libations; you can invite friends to join in too! Take your magazines and cut out any images and words that you feel are a part of your vision. You can also write appropriate words on your board.

Alternately, you can create a digital vision board and make sure it's accessible on your phone so that you can look at it everywhere you go. Two apps that are helpful for creating easy digital vision boards are Canva and Pinterest. Canva is for creating collages, and Pinterest is great because it helps you find images online. Another idea for your digital vision board: set it as your mobile wallpaper so that any time you look at your phone, you'll remember exactly what you're manifesting.

Month

Date/Day of Week

Moon Phase

_____ / _____ ◯

_____ / _____ ◯

_____ / _____ ◯

_____ / _____ ◯

_____ / _____ ◯

_____ / _____ ◯

_____ / _____ ◯

Week 5

Intention Setting

We set intentions so that all our attention can be directed at a singular thing. You must know what you want and why. Or, if you're not sure what you want yet, you need to ask yourself how you want to feel. Often, we think we want something, such as a big house or a soulmate, but really what we want is intangible: security, safety, love, comfort, joy. Begin by writing your intention below. You can also say it out loud. Say to yourself, "I want [this thing, person, or goal]" or however you'd like to phrase it. Sometimes, the thing that is meant for us is at the periphery of our understanding, so we call upon a Higher Intelligence to bring to us what is destined for us.

_____

_____

_____

_____

_____

_____

_____

_____

_____

_____

_____

Month

Date/Day of Week

Moon Phase

Week 6

Connect to a Higher Power

A Higher Power is a guiding protective power that helps us raise our awareness above and beyond our current circumstances. Connecting to this Higher Power will help you remember you're not only a part of this universal consciousness: you are it. You can connect with a Higher Power through meditation. Creating a personal altar with meaningful objects that can amplify your focus and intention is a wonderful way to do that. It can be a sacred space where you place favorite crystals, or photos of deities or ancestors (see also Week 8).

When you're ready to meditate, get comfortable. Close your eyes and take a deep breath in, hold it for a moment, then slowly exhale, allowing any tension to melt away. Bring your awareness to the top of your head; imagine a feeling of relaxation begin to spread through your body. Once you're entirely relaxed, envision an all-encompassing bright golden light emanating out from your heart space. You are safe and protected. Tune in to that energy of unconditional love within you. A loving presence. As you notice this presence, you may receive a message. Just focus on your intention and let the rest unfold. When you've connected to this presence long enough, bring your awareness back to your physical body.

Month

Date/Day of Week

Moon Phase

_____ /_____ ◯

_____ /_____ ◯

_____ /_____ ◯

_____ /_____ ◯

_____ /_____ ◯

_____ /_____ ◯

_____ /_____ ◯

Week 7

"Spiritual practice is not just sitting and meditation. Practice is looking, thinking, touching, drinking, eating, and talking. Every act, every breath, and every step can be practice and can help us to become more ourselves."

—Thich Nhat Hanh, *Your True Home*

Sadhana: A Daily Spiritual Practice

A daily devotion or spiritual practice is a time when you set an intention to quiet your mind. It's a time to notice and be aware of your inner world and the energy around you; to tap into the higher realms of your higher self, accessing your intuition to help guide you. Connecting to our higher self and this Higher Power puts us in the right space to let go of what's not in alignment with our vision and embrace who we need to be in order to manifest it. Listen and allow your heart and mind to open and allow what it is that needs to be birthed through your own consciousness. Create mindful rituals for your manifestation—for example, try setting a meditation schedule (see meditation technique in Week 6), drinking some tea before each intention-setting practice, or pulling some tarot cards for guidance before you settle in. List below rituals that might help you in your practice.

_____

_____

_____

_____

_____

_____

_____

_____

Month

_____

Date/Day of Week   **Moon Phase**

_____/_____   ◯

_____/_____   ◯

_____/_____   ◯

_____/_____   ◯

_____/_____   ◯

_____/_____   ◯

_____/_____   ◯

Week 8

"Thankfulness is the tune of angels."
—Attributed to Edmund Spenser

Devotional Offerings

To enhance your daily devotion ritual, try creating an offering for Mother Earth, your ancestors, deity, God, or Goddess. When I create my offerings, it's very simple: it's more about the intention and the energy that you give versus what you are offering. If it's a specific day like the spring or fall equinoxes, or the summer or winter solstices, I will buy special flowers for the occasion. I have a collection now of dried flowers that I save for offerings. On a new or full moon, I will offer the flowers to the earth as a gesture of gratitude. I will also say a little prayer for someone who needs it. We offer something because we are saying thank you for what we have received and what we are about to receive. Your offerings can be anything that is biodegradable. Write below some ideas of a special offering you could make today and why.

_____

_____

_____

_____

_____

_____

_____

_____

_____

_____

Month

Date/Day of Week   **Moon Phase**

_____ / _____   ○

_____ / _____   ○

_____ / _____   ○

_____ / _____   ○

_____ / _____   ○

_____ / _____   ○

_____ / _____   ○

Week 9

"The simultaneous occurrence of a certain psychic state
with one or more external events which appear
as meaningful parallels to the momentary subjective
state—and, in certain cases, vice-versa."
—Carl Jung, *Synchronicity*

Signs and Synchronicities

There is a magical thread that weaves through everything, creating patterns and synchronicities. I believe signs and synchronicities are ways that the other realms communicate with you, and that it's your job to decode them. Once you've set an intention, keep track of all the signs and synchronicities you notice, no matter how "crazy" they may seem. If you see a crow or notice the time is 11:11, write it down in this journal—especially if you see repeating patterns. If you notice the same person several times and you get an intuitive hit to introduce yourself, do it!

Some questions you can ask when you see synchronicities are: Why did I see this person or receive this information now? What was I thinking about at the time? How does it fit into my journey? Is it related to my intention? If you've noticed synchronicities lately, list them and try to answer these questions.

_____

_____

_____

_____

_____

_____

_____

_____

Month

Date/Day of Week   Moon Phase

Week 10

Start Where You Are

Your "reality" is a collection of so many things, in addition to the dreams and visions you are manifesting. Your reality includes your present moment: your relationships, socioeconomic status, ancestors' stories, intergenerational trauma. Take some time to think about your past and try to remember the times that you didn't pursue something that you loved because you were told not to or you weren't encouraged to.

Remember that you may feel that you have abandoned a part of yourself, but you can always recover it if you act with intention. Take a moment to identify a part of yourself that has been neglected and abandoned, and send kindness and attention to that part of your personality. Write down all the times that you can remember that you did something or made a decision about something based on security and safety. When did you choose fear over love?

_____

_____

_____

_____

_____

_____

_____

_____

_____

Month

Date/Day of Week

Moon Phase

Week 11

"They who dream by day are cognizant of many things which escape those who dream only by night."

—Edgar Allan Poe, *Eleonora*

Dream Discernment

For so much of our lives, we are told what to think and how to behave by our parents, teachers, mentors, and media. We are not taught to unlock our authentic selves. In childhood, we were not given the tools to understand who we are at the soul level. Ask yourself the following questions: What are your dreams? How do you see yourself living your life? Be totally honest with yourself. What comes up when you remove money, notoriety, and status from this situation? Whatever comes up, don't judge it. Write it down below and explore it.

_____

_____

_____

_____

_____

_____

_____

_____

_____

_____

_____

Month

Date/Day of Week

Moon Phase

Week 12

"The mutual practice of giving and receiving
is an everyday ritual when we know true love."
—bell hooks, *All About Love: New Visions*

Giving and Receiving

You can manifest anything you want by simply giving yourself wholeheartedly. You are a gift that you will give the Universe, and giving starts with radical authenticity: being completely honest with yourself about who you are and living in alignment with that truth—critical first steps toward manifesting. When your mind (thoughts and beliefs), heart (what you love), and soul (purpose) are in alignment, everything you do comes from a heart-centered place. When you're in this state, you'll have an abundance of energy and love to give freely and, in turn, you'll receive what you truly desire. These are some questions to ask yourself and answer below: What are you passionate about? What is a problem that you've solved that could be of service to other people? What have you overcome? What does it mean to live in alignment?

_____

_____

_____

_____

_____

_____

_____

_____

_____

_____

Month

Date/Day of Week

Moon Phase

Week 13

"To be who you are and become what you are capable of
is the only goal worth living."
—Alvin Ailey

Self-Worth and Love

Self-care does not just mean taking bubble baths, although that could be one act of self-care if it soaking will make you feel nurtured. Self-care is giving yourself the permission to be and do what you dream of, stand up for yourself, and ask for your worth. This is not selfish. This is necessary for you to feel whole. You can't give to others if you do not give to yourself first. When we know our worth, we don't allow ourselves to merely be victims of our circumstances. We take the leap, knowing that the net will appear. You must feel so full and whole that you have more than enough to give to others. You have an abundance of love, energy, and time, and the people around you get the benefits.

This exercise was developed by legendary spirituality writer Louise Hay. Stand in front of a mirror. Take a deep breath and repeat an affirmation to yourself ten times while you look into your eyes. Try: "I am worthy of everything I desire." You can also repeat any other affirmations that you feel called to.

Month

Date/Day of Week

Moon Phase

_____ / _____ ○

_____ / _____ ○

_____ / _____ ○

_____ / _____ ○

_____ / _____ ○

_____ / _____ ○

_____ / _____ ○

Week 14

"Realize deeply that the present moment is all you ever have."
—Eckhart Tolle, *The Power of Now*

Living in the Present Moment

Your life is a tapestry of interwoven moments that create the story of your own design. Here, in the present moment, is when you can experience serendipity and events that are beyond your wildest imagination, because you couldn't have planned them. We cannot move forward without being conscious of the present, and we can't be in the present if we keep looking back at the past. Tomorrow becomes now, and if we live in the past, it becomes our now instead. Time isn't linear—it's all happening simultaneously. Manifestation doesn't have to be years in the making. It can happen now. Learning to be in the present can be a lengthy process. So, set yourself up for success as you begin by doing an inventory here of your inputs and outputs in any given day. What are you reading or watching? Who are you interacting with?

_____

_____

_____

_____

_____

_____

_____

_____

_____

_____

_____

Month

Date/Day of Week

Moon Phase

_____ / _____ ○

_____ / _____ ○

_____ / _____ ○

_____ / _____ ○

_____ / _____ ○

_____ / _____ ○

_____ / _____ ○

Week 15

"Live being true to the single purpose of the moment."
—Yamamoto Tsunetomo, *Hagakure*

Digital Detox

Part of manifesting is being grateful for what you already have. When I'm in the present moment, I can fully appreciate everything that I currently have. If you're living in the past or projecting yourself into the future, you'll be living in scarcity. You may be surprised by the realizations you'll have when you focus on the now. A good first step is taking a one-day digital detox. Turn off your phone and TV; log off the laptop. The goal is to have little to no blue light exposure for one whole day. Notice how much mental space there is to think and create. Every time you reach for your phone or the remote, take a deep breath and feel yourself in the present moment. You'll find that the craving to scroll fades over the course of a day—it's hard at first but give it a try.

Note below the most difficult part of the detox. How did you spend the time that you weren't wired in?

_____

_____

_____

_____

_____

_____

_____

_____

_____

_____

Month

Date/Day of Week   **Moon Phase**

_____ / _____   ◯

_____ / _____   ◯

_____ / _____   ◯

_____ / _____   ◯

_____ / _____   ◯

_____ / _____   ◯

_____ / _____   ◯

Week 16

"And into the woods I go, to lose my mind and find my soul."
—Attributed to John Muir

Rewilding

Part of tuning in to creative energy is learning how to rewild ourselves—to sync back into natural cycles. It means retraining our bodies so that they know when to act and when to rest. It means re-establishing that there is a time to create, die, rebirth, and transform. The best way to heal your burnout and remind yourself to slow down is to be in nature. When you slow down, you can hear the inner calling of your soul. You can quiet your erratic mind and ground your energies to the Earth. The Earth reminds us of how abundance is all around us and inherently within us, as we are part of this Earth.

Spend some time outside, whether it be on your front porch or the middle of a forest, and consider the following: What does growth mean to you? Who will you be once you have grown, and what will you need to do to get there?

_____

_____

_____

_____

_____

_____

_____

_____

_____

Month

Date/Day of Week

Moon Phase

_____ / _____ ○

_____ / _____ ○

_____ / _____ ○

_____ / _____ ○

_____ / _____ ○

_____ / _____ ○

_____ / _____ ○

Week 17

"There is no way to repress pleasure
and expect liberation, satisfaction, or joy."

—Adrienne Maree Brown,
Pleasure Activism: The Politics of Feeling Good

Joy and Play

I believe we are closest to our manifestation and creative energy when we're having fun and when we're joyful. Perhaps you're thinking—consciously or subconsciously—that successful manifestation might require major effort. But I'm here to tell you that when you manifest successfully, the process is full of ease and joy. We must dispense with the belief that we are more worthy of something if we work hard for it. When we manifest, we desire something, and we want it to come into our lives. We often focus on a negative thing not being there. We focus on the *lack*, which perpetuates our feelings of scarcity.

When was the last time you were full of joy? Write about when you last forgot what time it was because you were so in the moment. When was the last time you were having so much fun that you didn't even look at your phone? What gets you excited?

_____

_____

_____

_____

_____

_____

_____

_____

Month

_____

Date/Day of Week   **Moon Phase**

_____ / _____ ◯

_____ / _____ ◯

_____ / _____ ◯

_____ / _____ ◯

_____ / _____ ◯

_____ / _____ ◯

_____ / _____ ◯

Week 18

> "All you can possibly need or desire is already yours.
> Call your desires into being by imagining and feeling
> your wish fulfilled."
>
> —Neville Goddard, *Feeling Is the Secret*

Act as If

To put it simply, the biggest part of manifestation is faith. Faith requires you to believe more in what you don't see than what you do see. You must believe without a shadow of a doubt that your life is changing, even though your environment and your surroundings might not yet show you the evidence of your manifestation. You see, if you can't even believe it's possible, then when you ask, you will automatically be filled with doubt. You don't have to be completely doubt-free, but you have to get to a place where you don't allow self-sabotage from your doubts to prevent you from being able to successfully manifest. Take a few moments to relax and meditate. When you come out of your meditation, write what you need to believe, feel, and do to bridge the gap to who you want to become. What do you need to let go of to become that version of you?

_____

_____

_____

_____

_____

_____

_____

_____

_____

Month

Date/Day of Week

Moon Phase

_____ / _____   ◯

_____ / _____   ◯

_____ / _____   ◯

_____ / _____   ◯

_____ / _____   ◯

_____ / _____   ◯

_____ / _____   ◯

Week 19

"You can never plan the future by the past."
—Edmund Burke

Honoring the Past

The historical past does not have to dictate your future. This is in no way excusing the things that happened to you, but to free yourself from the resentment, anger, and the heaviness that prevents us from transcending our own situation, we must let go. We are meant to flow with life and extract the wisdom from each experience, and to not hold on and define ourselves based on what happened in the past. To go through the death-and-rebirth phase, you'll have to let go of the parts of yourself that no longer fit the version of you that you need to become in order to manifest. I also like to call this the "phoenixing" moment when you metaphorically burn away the parts of you that you no longer need and then you are reborn from your ashes.

Write down a memory from the past that you can't let go of that you intend to let go of.

_____

_____

_____

_____

_____

_____

_____

_____

_____

_____

Month

Date/Day of Week

Moon Phase

/ ◯

/ ◯

/ ◯

/ ◯

/ ◯

/ ◯

/ ◯

Week 20

"The universe is change;
our life is what our thoughts make it."
—Marcus Aurelius, *Meditations*

Prepare for Change

Growth comes from discomfort. I hope you know this if you're going through a difficult time right now—you're are on the cusp of giving birth to a new beginning. Part of manifestation is trusting in the unknown—taking a leap into the Universe knowing that it will catch you without exactly understanding how. It's the Fool Card in tarot. It's when you have more belief in your vision than you do in your fears of the unknown. This is your invitation to let in that feeling and make the leap out into the dark without understanding quite what will happen when you get there.

Think back on a time when you were really scared about a potential change in your life. How did things work out? What did you learn from your experience? How does it impact your life today?

_____

_____

_____

_____

_____

_____

_____

_____

_____

_____

Month

Date/Day of Week

Moon Phase

_____ / _____   ◯

_____ / _____   ◯

_____ / _____   ◯

_____ / _____   ◯

_____ / _____   ◯

_____ / _____   ◯

_____ / _____   ◯

Week 21

Forgiveness

Like healing, forgiveness is not linear—and that's okay. Perhaps you thought you had forgiven and moved on from things that happened to you during childhood, but you were triggered unexpectedly, and you felt anger or fear or sadness when you thought you had released it long ago. When the triggers come back again, you might feel like you haven't fully healed yet or that you've failed at forgiving. Traumatic memories from childhood may resurface to help you soothe your inner child as an adult. Try your best not to run from these feelings: sit with them.

Write a letter to the person/people you want to forgive, including yourself.

_____

_____

_____

_____

_____

_____

_____

_____

_____

_____

Month

Date/Day of Week

Moon Phase

Week 22

"The subconscious mind is the 'sending station of the brain.'
... The creative imagination is the 'receiving set,' through
which the vibrations of thought are picked up from the ether."

—Napoleon Hill, *Think and Grow Rich*

Subconscious Programming

Our subconscious mind controls 95 percent of our behaviors but it's also very sensitive to suggestion. You can say all day long "I'm manifesting xyz," but if your subconscious mind isn't on board, then you won't manifest it. The mind and body are intimately connected. Thoughts transmitted via the mind's energy directly influence the physical body. It's important to be mindful of what you think about during this period, as well as what media you consume. Examine your reactions to the following lies we're often taught: You have to work hard to be rich. You need a college education to make money. You complete me. Manifestation works for some people but not me. These are just a few examples of things we may have taken in without realizing it.

Have you internalized any beliefs that are no longer serving you? How can you begin to investigate your subconscious with openness and curiosity? Explore this below.

_____

_____

_____

_____

_____

_____

_____

_____

_____

Month

Date/Day of Week

Moon Phase

Week 23

Sleep Programming

Right before you fall asleep, when your brain waves are moving more slowly, repeat to yourself one word or a mantra that represents what you are manifesting. Listen to positive affirmations or practice yoga nidra, a form of yoga that induces a deep state of conscious-awareness sleep. This state is deeper than simple relaxation and also allows you to be aware of your thoughts. In the morning, right when you wake up, write "morning pages." Morning pages is a practice from Julia Cameron's amazing book *The Artist's Way*. Cameron suggests that you free-write anything that comes up—don't stop or moderate yourself in any way. Essentially, what you're doing while completing morning pages is a form of channeling or downloading. As Dr. Joseph Murphy writes in *The Power of Your Subconscious Mind*, just before sleep or right after waking up in the morning is the best time to imprint new associations onto your subconscious mind.

Month

Date/Day of Week

Moon Phase

_____ / _____   ◯

_____ / _____   ◯

_____ / _____   ◯

_____ / _____   ◯

_____ / _____   ◯

_____ / _____   ◯

_____ / _____   ◯

Week 24

"Everyone carries a shadow, and the less it is embodied in the
individual's conscious life, the blacker and denser it is. . . .
It forms an unconscious snag, thwarting our most
well-meant intentions."
—Carl Jung

Shadow Work

The noted Swiss psychologist Carl Jung developed a number of influential
self-exploration concepts, including the "shadow self"—the basis for what's
called "shadow work." He believed that everyone has a shadow aspect and
integrating it into your conscious personality is important because it can
help you get past obstacles. Our shadows aren't bad, per se, we've just
deemed them unworthy and pushed them below the surface. It takes time
and effort to bring these parts of us back up, and it can be painful. There
are four basic steps in Jungian shadow work: 1. Accept the truth that our
shadow traits can't be repressed out of existence; 2. Take time for introspec-
tion and accept the root of each shadow trait; 3. Work to bring aspects of
these shadow traits into the light; 4. Allow shadow traits to express them-
selves in healthy ways.

What have you repressed? What do you hide in the shadows because
you thought it was bad?

_____

_____

_____

_____

_____

_____

_____

_____

Month

Date/Day of Week   **Moon Phase**

_____/_____   ◯

_____/_____   ◯

_____/_____   ◯

_____/_____   ◯

_____/_____   ◯

_____/_____   ◯

_____/_____   ◯

Week 25

"Never say never, because limits, like fears,
are often just an illusion."
—Michael Jordan, NBA Hall of Fame induction speech

Fear Setting

When my clients are crippled by anxiety and can't seem to take action, I ask them to either tell me all their fears or write them down. I learned this practice from author Tim Ferris. He recommends fear setting—moving toward your fears instead of away from them. As we've explored on this journey, human beings are more comfortable with the known than the unknown. To fear set, you write down your greatest fears and worst-case scenarios, as well as your backup plans. Once you write them down, you'll notice they'll immediately begin to seem less daunting, and often you'll realize right away how irrational they are. Fear setting is a great way to prove to yourself just how often your ego will tell you the different reasons why something will go wrong when it's just not true.

Write all your fears down. Which fears are you ready to release?

_____

_____

_____

_____

_____

_____

_____

_____

_____

_____

Month

Date/Day of Week

Moon Phase

_____/_____ ○

_____/_____ ○

_____/_____ ○

_____/_____ ○

_____/_____ ○

_____/_____ ○

_____/_____ ○

Week 26

"Healing is an art. It takes time.
It takes practice. It takes love."
—Pavana Reddy

Healing the Past

Healing is not linear. I see it as a spiral. I also see it as the ebbs and flows of life. Something might come back to trigger you that you thought you had already healed, but it might have come back in a different form. One thing to remember here is that you have more knowledge, experience, and wisdom this time around than when you did when you were first wounded. You're never at the same point on your healing journey, even if some days it might feel that way. Healing isn't always comfortable and it can be tough; it's a continuous journey. On the bright side, the more layers you peel away, the more liberated you'll feel. Do something healing for yourself. Take a bath, listen to beautiful music, make comforting food, talk to a friend, watch your favorite movie, or snuggle your pet. Resting also helps us tap into our creativity—consider taking some relaxing time and doing something expressive, like painting, crafting, singing, or dancing. Write below some ideas you have for incorporating healing, resting, and creativity into your life.

_____

_____

_____

_____

_____

_____

_____

_____

_____

Month

Date/Day of Week

Moon Phase

Week 27

"Healing is understanding how historical traumas
impact us across generations."

—Milagros Phillips, *Cracking the Healer's Code:
A Prescription for Healing Racism & Finding Wholeness*

Ancestral Healing

Many of us "fail" at manifesting because we are still carrying intergenerational trauma carried by our ancestors. Author and race healer Milagros Phillips says that you need two things to heal: (1) history and (2) being trauma-informed. We can only heal what we understand, and understanding our history and ancestral trauma will help us understand our own limiting beliefs and blocks. When our ancestors experienced a trauma they didn't fully process and resolve, it created epigenetic markers on DNA. These markers get passed down from generation to generation. If your parents are still with you, ask them the following questions and write about how their responses may have impacted you: How did you grow up? What was happening around you at the time? What were your parents' views on money, scarcity, and abundance? How did your parents get along? Did they ever argue? What were their dreams and did your parents pursue them? What was your life like before I came along?

_____

_____

_____

_____

_____

_____

_____

_____

Month

Date/Day of Week

Moon Phase

Week 28

"When I let go of what I am, I become what I might be.
When I let go of what I have, I receive what I need."
—Lao Tzu, *Tao Te Ching*

Release Ritual

Rituals are ways to mark the passage of time and to bring spiritual significance to important acts. Through this journey, you have made steps to honor and begin to understand your past. Just know that deep inside, all these experiences and lessons will always be a part of you, but a ritual is your vow to not live in them anymore. You are letting these things go, extracting the wisdom that you've learned and moving forward. *Transmutation* means "changing or altering matter in form, appearance, or nature" and especially indicates a transformation to a higher form. Imagine all the things you've written down being transmuted into energy that will be rebirthed into a new you. A release ritual can be anything from burning a piece of paper with your fears written on it to meditation. Write your own ritual below!

_____

_____

_____

_____

_____

_____

_____

_____

_____

_____

_____

Month

_____

Date/Day of Week   **Moon Phase**

_____ /_____   ◯

_____ /_____   ◯

_____ /_____   ◯

_____ /_____   ◯

_____ /_____   ◯

_____ /_____   ◯

_____ /_____   ◯

Week 29

Clearing Your Space

You have cut the cords of what was tethering you to negative emotions and experiences and now you can manifest from a different place—a more whole one. You are letting these things go, extracting the wisdom that you've learned and moving forward. Releasing your old story that bound you to the past and creating a different future for yourself is extremely cathartic. It may seem simple, but clean your physical space. Donate or throw away what you don't need. List below a few items you can get rid of that have "old" energy and write about the connection it has to your past:

_____

_____

_____

_____

_____

_____

_____

_____

_____

_____

_____

_____

_____

Month

_____

Date/Day of Week   **Moon Phase**

_____ / _____   ◯

_____ / _____   ◯

_____ / _____   ◯

_____ / _____   ◯

_____ / _____   ◯

_____ / _____   ◯

_____ / _____   ◯

Week 30

"Everything is energy and that's all there is to it.
Match the frequency of the reality you want and you
cannot help but get that reality."
—Darryl Anka

Chakra Energy

When you're manifesting, you're working with energy. Energy cannot be contained; it moves through us. You must learn to flow with it. I believe we all have a creative potential that lies within us, dormant, until we wake it up or activate it. First, we must have awareness that we have this potential energy and then we can use it to unleash the dormant creative potential within us, and therefore, manifest.

Working with chakras helps you tune in; it gives you more information when you're assessing your energy flow, which directly impacts how effective your active manifestations will be. (You can learn about chakras online, and I discuss them in more detail in *How to Manifest*.) For example, let's say I'm manifesting a creative project. I might discover an energy deficiency at my sacral chakra, where ideas are born, possibly indicating writer's block, apathy, or stagnancy. I can choose to focus my practices on the sacral chakra to balance it and open it up to the flow.

If you want to send healing energy to the centers that felt contracted or heavy, you can rub your palms together to activate Source energy. You don't have to be attuned to Reiki, but this is a Reiki technique. Set an intention of sending healing energy to a chakra or chakras. Place your hands on the chakra and focus your attention there, and then repeat in your mind your intention. When you are finished, give thanks to the Universe.

Month

Date/Day of Week

Moon Phase

_____ /_____ ○

_____ /_____ ○

_____ /_____ ○

_____ /_____ ○

_____ /_____ ○

_____ /_____ ○

_____ /_____ ○

Week 31

"There is one great truth on this planet: Whoever you are or whatever it is that you do, when you really want something, it's because that desire originated in the soul of the universe. It's your mission on Earth."

—Paulo Coelho, *The Alchemist*

Pleasure and Creation

Pleasure and eroticism do not just mean sex. They represent our ability to tap into our deep creative potential. Many people will say "I'm not creative!" but what they mean is that they don't resonate with traditional meanings ascribed to creativity such as skill in painting or creating music. But we are all creators. When you do the things you are passionate about, you allow the energy to flow. When you allow this energy to flow versus holding it in, you don't project those feelings out as lust or need. When you flow, you instead emit magnetism.

Spend time thinking about your own sexual and erotic energy. In the space below, consider the following: What would give me pleasure in terms of sight, touch, taste, smell, and hearing? What turns you on? What are your burning passions? How do you express them?

_____

_____

_____

_____

_____

_____

_____

_____

_____

Month

Date/Day of Week

Moon Phase

Week 32

The Law of Resonance

The Law of Resonance is what you attract based on an emotional response. It states that the rate of vibration projected will harmonize with and attract back energies with the same resonance. This determines whether you are in fear or love. Notice what is resonating with you at this time. Look at what you're attracting and see if it's something that you want to experience or not. Try not to judge yourself—energy can shift in an instant once you bring awareness to it. For example, if you only have friends around you who put you down and don't support you, you're not resonating on the frequency of love. If you want to attract supportive friends, this is an opportunity for you to ask yourself, "Why am I resonating below the frequency of love?" Maybe there's something internally that you have to pay attention to? Keep asking yourself, "How can I resonate more on the frequency of love?" You can always tune in to your Higher Power for guidance.

What is resonating with you now? What are you attracting? Do you want to retune the frequency?

_____

_____

_____

_____

_____

_____

_____

_____

_____

Month

Date/Day of Week

Moon Phase

_____ / _____ ◯

_____ / _____ ◯

_____ / _____ ◯

_____ / _____ ◯

_____ / _____ ◯

_____ / _____ ◯

_____ / _____ ◯

Week 33

Scripting

"Scripting" is a Law of Attraction technique where you write a new story about your life based on how you want it to be. You write your story as if it has already happened or is happening right now by focusing on how you would feel when your desires are manifested. The subconscious mind is malleable, and you can create new neural pathways. Please don't get discouraged if this takes time, because it took time to get you here and it will take the same amount of time to unwind some of your accumulated beliefs. Begin to write your new story below (in the present tense!) and consider the following: What time do you get up in the morning? Are you woken up by an alarm? Do you have a partner? Family? Pets? Where do you live? What does your home look like? You are getting ready for the day. What kind of clothes are you wearing? Do you work from home? How do you spend your day? What do you do for fun and pleasure? What kinds of adventures do you go on? What do you create?

_____

_____

_____

_____

_____

_____

_____

_____

_____

_____

Month

Date/Day of Week   **Moon Phase**

_____ / _____ ◯

_____ / _____ ◯

_____ / _____ ◯

_____ / _____ ◯

_____ / _____ ◯

_____ / _____ ◯

_____ / _____ ◯

Week 34

"I believe you can speak things into existence."
—Jay-Z, *Decoded*

Affirmations

When you speak words, something on the other side vibrates to match it and becomes attracted to you by the Law of Attraction. When spoken aloud, your words are spells. When you speak out to the Universe, you are performing an incantation. Similar to scripting and writing, you are *spelling*. In essence, affirmations are the way you communicate with your subconscious mind, taking responsibility for change and acknowledging your responsibility in what will happen.

Write below a few affirmations and practice saying them. Here are some examples: I am open to receiving, I am open to love, I am walking toward my abundance. I am healthy, I am beautiful, I am pure love and energy.

_____

_____

_____

_____

_____

_____

_____

_____

_____

_____

_____

_____

Month

_____

Date/Day of Week   **Moon Phase**

_____ / _____   ○

_____ / _____   ○

_____ / _____   ○

_____ / _____   ○

_____ / _____   ○

_____ / _____   ○

_____ / _____   ○

Week 35

"Water—the mighty, the pure, the beautiful,
the unfathomable."

—Letitia Elizabeth Landon, *The Book of Beauty*

Moon Water Intention Ritual

Water is a wonderful medium for purification, healing, and manifestation. Exposing yourself to this mutable, receptive element can bring you back into balance.

Plan to do this ritual on the new or full moon. (Make sure to wait if it is a void of course moon—the time when the moon makes its last aspect to when the moon changes signs; it's not a good time to set intentions or do a ritual. You can do search online for when the void of course moon is in connection to the moon phase during which you are doing your ritual.)

Get a glass jar or mason jar with a top, and fill it with water. Set up your ritual space. Clear the area energetically, or with local herbs or incense. Light a candle and meditate on your intention. Hold the glass jar of water between your hands. Take a deep inhale from the belly. Pause for a few seconds. Then exhale all the air out of your mouth. State your intention out loud. Feel the energy coming out of you through your hands. You can say a prayer to your water. At that point, you can either drink all of it in one sitting, or you can drink a sip each day for a week. If you have enough water, you can do this for fourteen days straight until the next moon phase.

Month

Date/Day of Week   **Moon Phase**

/   ◯
_____

/   ◯
_____

/   ◯
_____

/   ◯
_____

/   ◯
_____

/   ◯
_____

/   ◯
_____

Week 36

"Whatever you wish to manifest,
associate a feeling of love with it and impress that feeling
on the universal subconscious mind—and it will do the rest."
—Dr. Wayne Dyer, *Wishes Fulfilled*

Emotions: Energy in Motion

This week is all about separating thoughts from feelings and getting your emotional state into alignment with your vision. You can't necessarily change the way you feel, but you can filter your thoughts. You can reprogram your mind to elicit a feeling and emotion. Humans act on their feelings. When the feeling is powerful enough, you are mobilized to act, because action is necessary to create the life of your dreams and manifest. Thoughts alone are just concepts. However, we are not meant to cling onto these emotions. We need outlets, such as exercising, dancing, and breath work, through which we can channel our emotions. And if things get really overwhelming, don't rule out screaming! Emotional regulation happens when we choose to leave an emotional state—let's say, sadness or apathy.

Write down a few emotions you've been feeling lately and how you can release them.

_____

_____

_____

_____

_____

_____

_____

_____

_____

Month

Date/Day of Week

Moon Phase

_____ / _____ ○

_____ / _____ ○

_____ / _____ ○

_____ / _____ ○

_____ / _____ ○

_____ / _____ ○

_____ / _____ ○

Week 37

"All of our behavior results from the thoughts that precede it."
—Wayne Dyer, *You'll See It When You Believe It*

Thoughts vs. Feelings

In both psychology and energy healing, we talk about emotional regulation, which is what happens when we choose to leave an emotional state such as sadness or apathy. (Note, I'm not talking about mental illness. If you're dealing with something overwhelming that can't be resolved with energy healing techniques, please seek a licensed professional therapist.) You can emotionally regulate by reviewing your thoughts. What foods are you eating? What social media are you scrolling through? Who are you surrounding yourself with? These sources of stimuli may be impacting how you're feeling.

We can change our thoughts more easily than our emotions and behaviors. Changing our thoughts ignites a "feeling" response that will either motivate us or disempower us. Choose your thoughts wisely. Here is a technique to help you understand your thoughts versus your feelings: Observe your thought. What is the content? Is it true? Answer without judgment. What is the evidence of its validity? Move the thought of your head and into your body by dancing wildly to your favorite song! How do you feel now? Did any emotions surface? Are your feelings in alignment with your thoughts? Make notes below.

_____

_____

_____

_____

_____

_____

_____

_____

Month

Date/Day of Week

Moon Phase

_____ / _____ ○

_____ / _____ ○

_____ / _____ ○

_____ / _____ ○

_____ / _____ ○

_____ / _____ ○

_____ / _____ ○

Week 38

"It matters not what someone is born
but what they grow to be!"
—Albus Dumbledore in J. K. Rowling's
Harry Potter and the Goblet of Fire

Shifting Your Reality

Because our manifestations come from our state of mind, the quickest way to manifest is to *feel* as if what we desire is happening right now. Feel it now. Be happy now. Live in joy now. If you can imagine a version of yourself out there who is living your dream life in a parallel reality, tune in to that person's energy and start merging with that timeline. It's tough: when we manifest, we are intending to bring into our current life that which we do not currently have. Shifting your reality in this way can mess with your mind, because you'll want to see it to believe it, but remember: it's about believing first, and *then* you will see it.

These are prompts to help you determine what you need to think, believe, feel, and do to bridge the gap between the current you and the future you: What does the current you need to release to believe the future you is possible? What does the current you need to learn, read, and experience for you to get there?

_____

_____

_____

_____

_____

_____

_____

_____

_____

Month

Date/Day of Week

Moon Phase

Week 39

"The quest for wholeness can never begin
on the external level. It is always an inside job."
—Dr. Shefali Tsabary

Becoming Whole

It's likely that you want to manifest something because you feel that you aren't currently experiencing it. Conversely, you are experiencing the lack of it. What we default to is looking outside of ourselves to fill that lack. You will keep attracting your current state of mind unless you look within and heal this feeling of lack. How do you feel whole without the thing or person you're wishing for? Through joy, and the act of radiating that feeling out and into the world. The more joy you feel, the more whole and complete you'll feel, and that's the energy you will attract. The energy of joy activates our feeling of well-being and remember, well-being is wholeness.

Write below about what you are manifesting and what things in your life currently bring you joy.

_____

_____

_____

_____

_____

_____

_____

_____

_____

_____

Month

Date/Day of Week

Moon Phase

_____ / _____ ◯

_____ / _____ ◯

_____ / _____ ◯

_____ / _____ ◯

_____ / _____ ◯

_____ / _____ ◯

_____ / _____ ◯

Week 40

"Your conscience shouts, 'Here's what you should do,'
while your intuition whispers, 'Here's what you could do.'
Listen to that voice that tells you what you could do."
—Steven Spielberg, Harvard commencement address, 2016

Intuition

Your intuition is so important in the manifestation process: a well-developed sense of intuition will never steer you in the wrong direction, so it can help you know when your visions will bring you to the reality you desire, whether the Universe is sending you signs, and when to act based on those signs. The center of your intuition is the third eye: the ajna chakra. Practice this chant to activate your ajna chakra:

1. Sit in a comfortable meditation pose. Relax your body.
2. Take three deep breaths to bring yourself to your interior awareness.
3. On your next exhale, chant *aum*, slowly pronouncing each syllable: a-u-m.
4. Chant *aum* three times and afterward, sit in stillness and notice the vibration you have created.

Note below how you feel after this exercise.

_____

_____

_____

_____

_____

_____

_____

Month

Date/Day of Week   Moon Phase

_____ / _____ ◯

_____ / _____ ◯

_____ / _____ ◯

_____ / _____ ◯

_____ / _____ ◯

_____ / _____ ◯

_____ / _____ ◯

Week 41

"Once we achieve this balance, we will see everyone
as a balance of masculine and feminine. Everyone has a role.
Every energy is of equal value."

—Reena Kumarasingham, *The Magdalene Lineage:
Past Life Journeys into the Sacred Feminine Mysteries*

Yin and Yang

The Divine Feminine (yin) is space, darkness, chaos, softness, passivity, potential energy, age, infinity, and your subconscious mind. Like energy, the Divine Feminine is the foundation of all creation. It is the "is-ness" or the "being" of all things. In the West we were taught that when you want something, you go out and get it. That cause and effect is expressed through yang: masculine energy. But as we've learned, there is a time and place for taking action, and also a time in which the opposite is true. Yin is taking care of your mind, heart, body, and soul and preparing them to be the vessel that attracts the things to you. Maybe you're more comfortable with working and doing but not as familiar with the feminine energy of waiting, contemplating, and receiving. There must be an equal balance of feminine and masculine energy at all times and the discernment to know when to *be* versus *do*.

Chop wood, carry water. Today, stop worrying about getting the thing you want. Clean your bathroom. Buy groceries. Open your mail. Do the things that must be done. Take this time while you're "waiting" for your manifestation to arrive by living your life. Living in the moment puts you in the receptive mode and, if the proper detachment is achieved, paradoxically you will be ready for the next steps in the days to come.

Month

Date/Day of Week

Moon Phase

_____ / _____   ◯

_____ / _____   ◯

_____ / _____   ◯

_____ / _____   ◯

_____ / _____   ◯

_____ / _____   ◯

_____ / _____   ◯

Week 42

Finding Your Soul Family

When your manifestations start coming together and you start becoming the version of you that you've been calling in, you will rise above. In the process, you may even leave some people behind. If you don't feel supported by your friends, know that you can make new ones. Call in the energy that you want to experience. You should be around people who you admire: who are smarter than you, who have talents that you find amazing, who seem to have unending bravery and strength. When you are around people you respect and look up to, you will rise to the occasion simply by osmosis. And when you need a support system to back you up when the going gets tough, you will have the best you can possibly imagine.

List all of your closest friends, particularly those in your inner circle, and meditate on whether those relationships are reciprocal.

_____

_____

_____

_____

_____

_____

_____

_____

_____

_____

Month

Date/Day of Week

Moon Phase

Week 43

"If the thought of lack . . . has become part of who you think you are, you will always experience lack rather than acknowledge the good that is already in your life. . . . Acknowledging the good that is already in your life is the foundation for all abundance."

—Eckhart Tolle, *A New Earth*

Healing Your Scarcity Mentality

For most of us who start on the manifestation journey, we begin because we want something that we feel that we don't have. In essence, we start manifesting from a place of lack. But the Universe doesn't care about what you want: it reacts to vibration, so if you are manifesting from a place of lack, it will keep giving you the same vibration you currently have until you change it. When your mind is trapped in a scarcity mentality, you believe that the world cannot provide for us all. We were taught to believe in lack, we can unlearn it. Tune in to your thoughts, beliefs, and feelings. Try not to judge what comes through and ask yourself, are you manifesting from a place of lack? Awareness is key.

What do you feel like you're lacking? Look at what you're manifesting and ask yourself, what will this bring to my life? How can I fill that void now with the resources I have?

_____

_____

_____

_____

_____

_____

_____

_____

Month

Date/Day of Week   **Moon Phase**

_____ / _____ ◯

_____ / _____ ◯

_____ / _____ ◯

_____ / _____ ◯

_____ / _____ ◯

_____ / _____ ◯

_____ / _____ ◯

Week 44

"Abundance is about being rich, with or without money."
—Attributed to Suze Orman

Cultivating an Abundance Mindset

Manifestation based on abundance leads to creativity, love, reciprocal intimate relationships, and generative opportunities that will bring you to joy. Ultimately, what you're manifesting is becoming an open channel to have an abundance of opportunities and creative ideas, which will help you to create the life that you want. Abundance means truly being in the flow. Your value is not contingent on what you do or how you make money. The value that you bring to this world is just being you. What do you define as an abundant life? Every time you experience abundance, take a moment and acknowledge it. Keep track of all the forms of abundance you witness in your Notes app, or by hand in this planner.

What are some forms of abundance you've witnessed recently? This can be anything from a beautiful sunset or a hug to a cute puppy video or laughing with a friend. Don't limit yourself! Everything, big or small, is worth noting in this list.

_____

_____

_____

_____

_____

_____

_____

_____

_____

_____

Month

_____

Date/Day of Week   **Moon Phase**

_____ / _____   ◯

_____ / _____   ◯

_____ / _____   ◯

_____ / _____   ◯

_____ / _____   ◯

_____ / _____   ◯

_____ / _____   ◯

Week 45

"Everything that happens in the universe
begins with intention."
—Deepak Chopra

Focus on Your Values

The Tower Card in tarot tells us that if you build your life on shaky ground, it will inevitably fall apart. That archetypal image is just common sense when it comes to manifestation: you should build on a solid foundation because that means you've already laid the groundwork for your prosperity. Your foundation in this case is your intention. Your whole life is a manifestation and a creation of your beliefs about yourself.

Consider the following questions below: What do you really value? How do you spend your time and money, and how would you like to? What are your three most important core values?

_____

_____

_____

_____

_____

_____

_____

_____

_____

_____

_____

_____

Month

Date/Day of Week

Moon Phase

_____ / _____ ○

_____ / _____ ○

_____ / _____ ○

_____ / _____ ○

_____ / _____ ○

_____ / _____ ○

_____ / _____ ○

Week 46

"The mindset isn't about seeking a result—it's more about
the process of getting to that result. It's about the journey
and the approach. It's a way of life."
—Kobe Bryant, *The Mamba Mentality: How I Play*

Take Inspired Action

Knowledge is useless without application. Manifestation as a concept won't
lead you to what you desire. I don't want you to just absorb the information
in these pages without creating real change. Action does not always mean
what we think it means: action can be yin, and you could interpret that to
mean resting and taking care of yourself. Note that manifesting the thing
that you want is the first step. But you also need to know how to hold it
once it exists. For example, you might be manifesting money, but once you
get the money, what action steps will you take in terms of investing it? The
manifestation process isn't just the act of bringing dreams into reality—you
need a solid, grounded approach to hold this energy.

Take one action specific to your manifestation. If you are manifesting
money, learn about investing, so that when you get the wealth you are seeking, you can maintain it. Write about what your next step toward manifesting your goal will be.

_____

_____

_____

_____

_____

_____

_____

_____

Month

_____

Date/Day of Week   **Moon Phase**

_____ / _____ ○

_____ / _____ ○

_____ / _____ ○

_____ / _____ ○

_____ / _____ ○

_____ / _____ ○

_____ / _____ ○

Week 47

"Love is quivering happiness."
—Kahlil Gibran

Love: The Most Powerful Force in the Universe

Unconditional love is what binds everything in the Universe together. It is all-encompassing Source energy. When you love yourself and your life, you become magnetic: Everything and everyone is drawn to your energy. The way to align with love is to do the things you love, and add love to everything you do—even the stuff that seems boring but necessary. When you take responsibility for co-creating your life with the Universe, you are manifest every day through your decisions and how you spend your time. To love your life is to truly live it.

Every year, I create a bucket list of things that I want to do. I resolve to do them with or without other people because I won't wait for someone to live my life. However, life is always more fun with friends and family so if you can do this with others, please do! Create a bucket list of things you can do this year by yourself or with friends!

_____

_____

_____

_____

_____

_____

_____

_____

_____

_____

Month

Date/Day of Week

Moon Phase

Week 48

"When I started counting my blessings,
my whole life turned around."
—Willie Nelson

Gratitude

Gratitude is thanking the Universe in advance for your blessing. Give gratitude for your manifestations before they arrive, because it tricks your subconscious mind into thinking that you already have what you're envisioning. It's also a great way to celebrate your wins, both big and small. Don't wait for accolades and promotions to give gratitude—every moment is an excellent chance to celebrate the fact that you're alive. What you focus on expands, so instead of focusing all your attention on what you lack, focus on what you have today. Send love and blessings to that thing or person. Remember that giving and receiving are one and the same.

List all of the things and people you are grateful for and then read your list out loud. Make sure to tell people how you feel about them.

_____

_____

_____

_____

_____

_____

_____

_____

_____

_____

Month

Date/Day of Week

Moon Phase

Week 49

"If you look too closely at the form, you miss the essence."
—Attributed to Rumi

Detachment

Wanting too hard is a very common misstep, and everyone does it. When you focus on yourself and do the work, what is meant for you will find you. When we are too attached to form—how something should look—we will not be aware enough to see what's right in front of us. Always remind yourself that you need to focus on the essence—the feeling as opposed to the form. Our minds are often the very things that hold us back from "seeing" our manifestations because we are too busy waiting for what we expect. The moment you surrender, the resistance releases, and your manifestation often comes in. Instead of asking the Universe, "is this going to happen?" I invite you to ask instead, "how can I make this happen with what is in my control?"

Write below steps within your control that you can take right now on your journey to manifestation.

_____

_____

_____

_____

_____

_____

_____

_____

_____

_____

Month

_____

Date/Day of Week   **Moon Phase**

_____ / _____   ◯

_____ / _____   ◯

_____ / _____   ◯

_____ / _____   ◯

_____ / _____   ◯

_____ / _____   ◯

_____ / _____   ◯

Week 50

"A burning passion coupled with
absolute detachment is the key to all success."
—Mahatma Gandhi

Detachment Meditation

You've connected yourself to universal love and spent time loving yourself
and your life. You've also celebrated and gave gratitude. Now it's time to
detach from the outcome: simply sit back and allow the Universe to bring it
to you. You can do this by reminding yourself to connect to the essence of
your desire as opposed to the form. Perform the following meditation and
write about your experience:

Close your eyes. Feel your sits bones rooted down to the chair or floor
beneath you. Feel the crown of the head rooting up to the heart of the sky.
Feel expansive in your physical body and your energetic body. Allow the
release of any tension. Notice where you feel contracted, and let it go with
your breath. Inhale through your nose to the count of 4 and exhale for the
count of 4. Repeat this for 1 minute. Bring into focus what you're manifesting right now. Visualize it as if it's happening right now. Conjure up all the
images you need to, to get you there.

What does it feel like to have this manifestation into your life now?

_____

_____

_____

_____

_____

_____

_____

_____

Month

_____

Date/Day of Week   **Moon Phase**

_____ / _____ ○

_____ / _____ ○

_____ / _____ ○

_____ / _____ ○

_____ / _____ ○

_____ / _____ ○

_____ / _____ ○

Week 51

"Trust me, I know what I'm doing."
—The Universe

You Are Divinely Protected

You are never given what you're not ready for. That means that if you don't receive your manifestation on your timeline, you're being protected, because either something better is coming along or your timing isn't right. The manifestation process is also about building a relationship and trust with the Divine Power you can't always access or experience directly. Trust that it has your best interest at heart. You may be feeling frustrated that your manifestations have not begun to show up in the physical world. If they haven't come in yet, contemplate the following below: Do you feel abundant? Do you feel whole? Do you feel love? Do you feel rich? If the answer is no to any of those questions, then go deeper. Go back to a previous week or day and start again, not with anger, but with gratitude for the time you are giving yourself, and for the divine forces that will be guiding you.

_____

_____

_____

_____

_____

_____

_____

_____

_____

_____

Month

Date/Day of Week

Moon Phase

Week 52

"To make the future demands courage.
It demands work. But it also demands faith."
—Peter F. Drucker

Faith and Trust

Many of us were taught that if we want something, we have to go out and get it ourselves, but there's so much that you can't control. This week is about having faith and trust. Affirm to the Universe that you are here and have given yourself over to the process of creation. You have detached from the outcome and are ready to step back and let it do its part. Manifestation requires trust and a radical vision. The root word for *radical* is *root*. It comes from something deep within you. When you planted those intentions during the first week, trust that there are roots firmly planted into the soil of your subconscious mind. With daily care, watering, and sunshine, the fruit will come when the timing is right. Creating a tangible representation of your co-creative abilities will be rewarding and cathartic. You are creating an art piece inspired by what you're manifesting for your life. Remind yourself of your visions, intentions, and imagination. You can choose any medium that you like. Painting, drawing, charcoal, colored pencils, mixed media, sculpture, the sky's the limit! Share your experiences and stories with others. When you have the courage to stand in your truth, you encourage others to do the same.

Month

Date/Day of Week   **Moon Phase**

_____ / _____   ○

_____ / _____   ○

_____ / _____   ○

_____ / _____   ○

_____ / _____   ○

_____ / _____   ○

_____ / _____   ○

Notes

About the Author

LAURA CHUNG is a Reiki master, yoga teacher, astrologer, and the host of two podcasts, *Awaken and Align* and *The Werk*. She is the author of *How to Manifest: Make Your Dreams a Reality in 40 Days*. Laura has her Master of Science in Industrial and Organizational Psychology. She is an activist and trauma-informed healer who uses her various media platforms to share spiritual wisdom and decolonial education toward collective healing and liberation. She uses her intuitive and psychic abilities to help people unlearn harmful programming and remember their soul print, their soul's truth and destiny. Laura's intention is to help people manifest the life of their dreams.

Social media: @iamlaurachung
Podcasts: Awaken and Align, The Werk
Website: Laurakchung.com